Animal Lovi

Give Baby a security blanket that's also a cuddly companion!
These sweet lovies are adorable when you want to make a handmade gift
for granchildern or a special baby shower. Choose from 10 designs.

2

5

8

10

13

16

18

21

24

26

LEISURE ARTS, INC. • Maumelle, Arkansas

Brown Bear

◼◼◻◻ **EASY +**

Approximate Finished Size: Blanket - 12" (30.5 cm) square

SHOPPING LIST

Yarn (Medium Weight)

[3.5 ounces, 170 yards
(100 grams, 156 meters) per skein]:

☐ Brown - 1 skein

☐ Tan - small amount

Knitting Needles

Straight,

☐ Size 9 (5.5 mm) (for Blanket)

Double pointed (set of 4),

☐ Size 8 (5 mm) (for Head, Ears,
and Arms)

Additional Supplies

☐ Split ring marker

☐ Polyester fiberfill

☐ Black embroidery floss

☐ Red embroidery floss

☐ Tapestry needle

☐ Yarn needle

TECHNIQUES USED

▶ YO *(Fig. 2, page 30)*

▶ M1 *(Figs. 3a & b, page 30)*

▶ K2 tog *(Fig. 4, page 30)*

INSTRUCTIONS
Blanket

With straight knitting needles and
Brown, cast on 4 sts.

Row 1: Knit across.

Row 2 (Right side)**:** K2, YO, K2: 5 sts.

Increase Row: K2, YO, knit across:
6 sts.

Repeat Increase Row until you have
62 sts on the needle.

Decrease Row: K1, K2 tog, YO, K2 tog,
knit across: 61 sts.

Repeat Decrease Row until you have 5 sts left on the needle.

Last Row: K1, K2 tog, K2: 4 sts.

Bind off all sts in **knit**.

Head

With double pointed needles, using Brown and leaving an 8" (20.5 cm) end to close cast on opening, cast on 6 sts; divide sts onto 3 needles *(see Using Double Pointed Needles, page 30)*; place a marker to indicate the beginning of the round *(see Markers, page 29)*.

Rnds 1 and 2: Knit around.

Rnd 3 (Increase rnd)**:** (K1, M1) around: 12 sts.

Rnd 4: Knit around.

Rnds 5 and 6: Repeat Rnds 3 and 4: 24 sts.

Rnd 7: (K2, M1) around: 36 sts.

Thread yarn needle with beginning end and weave through cast on edge; pull **tightly** to close opening, then secure end inside Head.

Rnds 8-11: Knit around.

Rnd 12: (K2, K2 tog) around: 27 sts.

Rnd 13: Knit around.

Rnd 14 (Decrease rnd)**:** (K1, K2 tog) around: 18 sts.

Rnd 15: Knit around.

Stuff Head lightly with polyester fiberfill.

Rnds 16 and 17: Repeat Rnds 14 and 15: 12 sts.

Rnd 18: K2 tog around; cut yarn leaving a 12" (30.5 cm) end for sewing: 6 sts.

To gather the remaining sts, thread yarn needle with the end and slip the remaining sts onto the yarn needle and yarn; pull **tightly** to close the hole, then secure end, leaving the end long to sew to Blanket later.

Arm (Make 2)

With double pointed needles, using Tan and leaving an 8" (20.5 cm) end to close cast on opening, cast on 11 sts; place a marker to indicate the beginning of the round.

Rnds 1 and 2: Knit around; at end of Rnd 2, cut Tan.

Rnds 3-12: With Brown, knit around.

Bind off all sts in **knit**, leaving a long end for sewing.

Close cast on opening with beginning end.

Stuff Arm lightly with polyester fiberfill.

Finishing

Using photo as a guide:
With 📹 outline stitch and Black floss *(Figs. 7a & b, page 31)*, add U-shaped eyes to Head.
With 📹 straight stitch and Red floss *(Fig. 9, page 31)*, add remaining facial features.
With long end from Outer Ear, sew Ears to Head.
Flatten top of Arms and sew to each side of Head with long end.
With long end, sew Head to center of Blanket.

Ear (Make 2)
OUTER

With double pointed needles, using Brown and leaving an 8" (20.5 cm) end to close cast on opening, cast on 7 sts; place a marker to indicate the beginning of the round.

Rnd 1 (Right side)**:** Knit around.

Rnd 2: (K1, M1) around: 14 sts.

Close cast on opening with beginning end.

Rnd 3: Knit around.

Bind off all sts in **knit**, leaving a long end for sewing Ear to Head.

INNER

With double pointed needles, using Tan and leaving an 8" (20.5 cm) end to close cast on opening, cast on 6 sts; place a marker to indicate the beginning of the round.

Rnd 1 (Right side)**:** Knit around.

Rnd 2: (K1, M1) around: 12 sts.

Close cast on opening with beginning end.

Rnd 3: Knit around.

Bind off all sts in **knit**, leaving a long end for sewing Inner Ear to Outer Ear.

Thread yarn needle with long end. With **wrong** sides together, sew Inner Ear to Outer Ear.

Bunny

EASY +

Approximate Finished Size: Blanket - 12" (30.5 cm) square

TECHNIQUES USED

▶ M1 (*Figs. 3a & b, page 30*)

▶ K2 tog (*Fig. 4, page 30*)

INSTRUCTIONS

Blanket

With straight knitting needles and White, cast on 51 sts.

Row 1 (Wrong side): K2, P1, (K1, P1) across to last 2 sts, K2.

Rows 2 and 3: K3, P1, (K1, P1) across to last 3 sts, K3.

Rows 4 and 5: K2, P1, (K1, P1) across to last 2 sts, K2.

Repeat Rows 2-5 for pattern until piece measures approximately 12" (30.5 cm) from cast on edge, ending by working a **right** side row.

Bind off all sts in **knit**.

Head

With White, work same as Brown Bear, page 3.

Ear (Make 2)

Outer and Inner Ear are worked in rows on 2 double pointed needles.

OUTER

With double pointed needles, using White and leaving an 8" (20.5 cm) end to sew Ear to Head, cast on 4 sts.

Rows 1 and 2: Knit across.

Row 3: K2, M1, K2: 5 sts.

Rows 4-6: Knit across.

Row 7: K2, M1, K1, M1, K2: 7 sts.

Rows 8 and 9: Knit across.

Row 10: K1, (K2 tog, K1) twice: 5 sts.

Row 11: K1, K2 tog twice: 3 sts.

Row 12: K1, K2 tog: 2 sts.

Row 13: K2 tog: one st.

Cut yarn leaving a 4" (10 cm) end; draw end through remaining st to secure.

INNER

With double pointed needles, using Pink and leaving a 10" (25.5 cm) end to sew Inner Ear to Outer Ear, cast on 4 sts.

Rows 1 and 2: Knit across.

Row 3: K2, M1, K2: 5 sts.

Rows 4 and 5: Knit across.

Row 6: K2, M1, K1, M1, K2: 7 sts.

Rows 7 and 8: Knit across.

Row 9: K1, (K2 tog, K1) twice: 5 sts.

Row 10: K1, K2 tog twice: 3 sts.

Row 11: K1, K2 tog: 2 sts.

Bind off remaining sts in **knit**.

Thread yarn needle with long end and sew Inner Ear to Outer Ear.

Arm (Make 2)

With double pointed needles, using White and leaving an 8" (20.5 cm) end to close cast on opening, cast on 11 sts; place a marker to indicate the beginning of the round.

Rnds 1-13: Knit around.

Bind off all sts in **knit**, leaving a long end for sewing.

Close cast on opening with beginning end.

Stuff Arm lightly with polyester fiberfill.

Carrot

With double pointed needles, using Orange and leaving an 8" (20.5 cm) end to close cast on opening, cast on 6 sts; place a marker to indicate the beginning of the round.

Rnds 1 and 2: Knit around.

Rnd 3: K2, (M1, K2) twice: 8 sts.

Rnd 4: Knit around.

Rnd 5: K2, (M1, K3) twice: 10 sts.

Rnd 6: Knit around.

Close cast on opening with beginning end.

Rnd 7: K2, (K2 tog, K2) twice: 8 sts.

Rnd 8: (K1, K2 tog) twice, K2: 6 sts.

Stuff Carrot very lightly with polyester fiberfill.

Rnd 9: Knit around.

Rnd 10: K2 tog around: 3 sts.

Cut yarn leaving a long end for sewing. Thread yarn needle with the end and slip the remaining sts onto the yarn needle and yarn; pull **tightly** to close the hole and secure end.

Cut three 6" (15 cm) pieces of Green yarn. Thread yarn needle with one length and insert through top of Carrot (at base of Rnd 1). Tie yarn in a knot. Repeat with remaining lengths.

Finishing

Using photo as a guide:
With outline stitch and Brown floss *(Figs. 7a & b, page 31)*, add U-shaped eyes to Head.
With straight stitch and Pink floss *(Fig. 9, page 31)*, add remaining facial features.
With long end from Outer Ear, sew Ears to Head.
Flatten top of Arms and sew to each side of Head with long end.
Sew Carrot to one of the Arms.
With long end, sew Head to center of Blanket.

Lamb

Approximate Finished Size: Blanket - 12" (30.5 cm) square

SHOPPING LIST

Yarn (Medium Weight) ④

[3 ounces, 197 yards
(85 grams, 180 meters) per skein]:
☐ Natural - 1 skein
☐ Grey - 1 skein
(Super Bulky Weight) ⑥
[5 ounces, 125 yards
142 grams, 114 meters) per skein]:
☐ Tan - 1 skein

Knitting Needles

Straight,
☐ Size 9 (5.5 mm) (for Blanket)
Double pointed (set of 4),
☐ Size 8 (5 mm) (for Head, Ears, and Arms)

Additional Supplies

☐ Split ring marker
☐ Polyester fiberfill
☐ Brown embroidery floss
☐ Tapestry needle
☐ Yarn needle

TECHNIQUES USED

🎥 M1 *(Figs. 3a & b, page 30)*
🎥 K2 tog *(Fig. 4, page 30)*

INSTRUCTIONS
Blanket

With straight needles and Natural, cast on 52 sts.

Rows 1-3: Knit across.

Row 4 (Wrong side)**:** K1, purl across to last st, K1.

Rows 5-9: K6, P5, (K5, P5) across to last st, K1.

Rows 10-16: K1, P5, (K5, P5) across to last 6 sts, K6.

Row 17: Knit across.

Repeat Row 17 until piece measures approximately 9" (23 cm) from cast on edge, ending by working a **right** side row.

Next 6 Rows: K1, P5, (K5, P5) across to last 6 sts, K6.

Next 5 Rows: K6, P5, (K5, P5) across to last st, K1.

Last 3 Rows: Knit across.

Bind off all sts in **knit**.

Head

With Grey, work same as Brown Bear, page 3, through Rnd 10; at end of Rnd 10, cut Grey: 36 sts.

With Tan and beginning with Rnd 11, complete same as Brown Bear.

Ear (Make 2)

Ear is worked in rows on 2 double pointed needles.

With double pointed needles, using Tan and leaving an 8" (20.5 cm) end to sew Ear to Head, cast on 5 sts.

Rows 1 and 2: Knit across.

Row 3: (K2, M1) twice, K1: 7 sts.

Row 4: Knit across.

Row 5: K1, (K2 tog, K1) twice: 5 sts.

Row 6: Knit across.

Row 7: K1, K2 tog, K2: 4 sts.

Row 8: Knit across.

Row 9: K2 tog twice: 2 sts.

Bind off remaining sts in **knit**.

Arm (Make 2)

With double pointed needles, using Tan and leaving an 8" (20.5 cm) end to close cast on opening, cast on 8 sts; place a marker to indicate the beginning of the round.

Rnds 1-13: Knit around.

Bind off all sts in **knit**, leaving a long end for sewing.

Close cast on opening with beginning end.

Stuff Arm lightly with polyester fiberfill.

Finishing

Using photo as a guide:
With 🎥 outline stitch and Brown floss *(Figs. 7a & b, page 31)*, add U-shaped eyes to Head.
With 🎥 straight stitch and Brown floss *(Fig. 9, page 31)*, add remaining facial features.
Fold cast on edge of each Ear in half and sew to Head with long end.
Flatten top of Arms and sew to each side of Head with long end.
Thread yarn needle with a 12" (30.5 cm) length of Grey and sew Head to center of Blanket.

Penguin

EASY +

Approximate Finished Size:

Blanket - 12" (30.5 cm) square

Yarn (Medium Weight)

[3.5 ounces, 170 yards
(100 grams, 156 meters) per skein]:

☐ White - 1 skein

☐ Black - 1 skein

Knitting Needles

Straight,

☐ Size 9 (5.5 mm) (for Blanket)

Double pointed (set of 4),

☐ Size 8 (5 mm) (for Head, Eye
   Patches, and Wings)

Additional Supplies

☐ Split ring marker

☐ Polyester fiberfill

☐ Black embroidery floss

☐ Orange embroidery floss

☐ Tapestry needle

☐ Yarn needle

TECHNIQUES USED

🎥 YO *(Fig. 2, page 30)*

🎥 M1 *(Figs. 3a & b, page 30)*

🎥 K2 tog *(Fig. 4, page 30)*

INSTRUCTIONS

Blanket

With White, work same as Brown Bear, page 3.

Head

🎥 With double pointed needles, using Black and leaving an 8" (20.5 cm) end to close cast on opening, cast on 7 sts; divide sts onto 3 needles *(see Using Double Pointed Needles, page 30)*; place a marker to indicate the beginning of the round *(see Markers, page 29)*.

Rnds 1 and 2: Knit around.

Rnd 3 (Increase rnd): (K1, M1) around: 14 sts.

Rnd 4: Knit around.

Rnds 5 and 6: Repeat Rnds 3 and 4: 28 sts.

Rnd 7: (K2, M1) around: 42 sts.

Thread yarn needle with beginning end and weave through cast on edge; pull **tightly** to close opening, then secure end inside Head.

Rnds 8-11: Knit around.

Rnd 12 (Decrease rnd): (K1, K2 tog) around: 28 sts.

Rnd 13: Knit around.

Rnd 14: (K2, K2 tog) around: 21 sts.

Rnd 15: Knit around.

Stuff Head lightly with polyester fiberfill.

Rnds 16 and 17: Repeat Rnds 12 and 13: 14 sts.

Rnd 18: K2 tog around; cut yarn leaving a 12" (30.5 cm) end for sewing: 7 sts.

📹 To gather the remaining sts, thread the yarn needle with the end and slip the remaining sts onto the yarn needle and yarn; pull **tightly** to close the hole, then secure end, leaving the end long to sew to Blanket later.

Eye Patch (Make 2)

With double pointed needles, using White and leaving an 8" (20.5 cm) end to close cast on opening, cast on 6 sts; place a marker to indicate the beginning of the round.

Rnd 1 (Right side): Knit around.

Rnd 2: (K1, M1) around: 12 sts.

Bind off all sts in **knit**, leaving a long end to sew to Head.

Close cast on opening with beginning end.

Wing (Make 2)

Wing is worked in rows on 2 double pointed needles.

With double pointed needles, using Black and leaving an 8" (20.5 cm) end to sew Wing to Head, cast on 5 sts.

Rows 1 and 2: Knit across.

Row 3: K1, M1, K3, M1, K1: 7 sts.

Rows 4 and 5: Knit across.

Row 6: K1, (K2 tog, K1) twice: 5 sts.

Rows 7 and 8: Knit across.

Row 9: K1, K2 tog, K2: 4 sts.

Row 10: Knit across.

Row 11: K2 tog twice: 2 sts.

Bind off remaining sts in **knit**.

Finishing

Using photo as a guide:
With 📹 outline stitch and Black floss *(Figs. 7a & b, page 31)*, add U-shaped eyes to Eye Patches.
With long end, sew Eye Patches to Head.
With 📹 straight stitch and Orange floss *(Fig. 9, page 31)*, add upside-down triangle for beak; then fill triangle with 📹 satin stitch *(Fig. 8, page 31)*.
With long end, sew Wings to each side of Head.
With long end, sew Head to center of Blanket.

Duck

EASY +

Approximate Finished Size: Blanket - 12" (30.5 cm) square

SHOPPING LIST

Yarn (Medium Weight)

[3.5 ounces, 170 yards
(100 grams, 156 meters) per skein]:
☐ Yellow - 1 skein
☐ White - small amount

Knitting Needles

Straight,
☐ Size 9 (5.5 mm) (for Blanket)
Double pointed (set of 4),
☐ Size 8 (5 mm) (for Head &
   Wings)

Additional Supplies

☐ Split ring marker
☐ Polyester fiberfill
☐ Brown embroidery floss
☐ Scrap piece of Orange felt
☐ Matching thread & needle
☐ Tapestry needle
☐ Yarn needle

TECHNIQUES USED

🎥 M1 *(Figs. 3a & b, page 30)*
🎥 K2 tog *(Fig. 4, page 30)*

INSTRUCTIONS

Blanket

With straight knitting needles and Yellow, cast on 48 sts.

Row 1 (Right side)**:** (K1, P1) across.

Row 2: (P1, K1) across.

Rows 3-8: Repeat Rows 1 and 2, 3 times.

Row 9: K1, P1, knit across to last 3 sts, P1, K1, P1.

Row 10: P1, K1, purl across to last 3 sts, K1, P1, K1.

Rows 11-20: Repeat Rows 9 and 10, 5 times.

Cut Yellow.

Rows 21-42: With White, repeat Rows 9 and 10, 11 times.

Cut White.

Rows 43-55: With Yellow, repeat Rows 9 and 10, 6 times; then repeat Row 9 once **more**.

Row 56: (P1, K1) across.

Row 57: (K1, P1) across.

Rows 58-62: Repeat Rows 56 and 57 twice, then repeat Row 56 once **more**.

Bind off all sts in pattern.

Head

With Yellow, work same as Penguin, page 11.

Wing (Make 2)

Wing is worked in rows on 2 double pointed needles.

With double pointed needles, using Yellow and leaving an 8" (20.5 cm) end to sew Wing to Head, cast on 5 sts.

Rows 1 and 2: Knit across.

Row 3: K1, M1, K3, M1, K1: 7 sts.

Rows 4 and 5: Knit across.

Row 6: K1, (K2 tog, K1) twice: 5 sts.

Rows 7 and 8: Knit across.

Row 9: K1, K2 tog, K2: 4 sts.

Row 10: Knit across.

Row 11: K2 tog twice: 2 sts.

Bind off remaining sts in **knit**.

Finishing

Using photo as a guide:

With 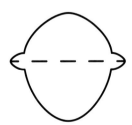 outline stitch and Brown floss *(Figs. 7a & b, page 31)*, add U-shaped eyes.

Trace diagram of Beak and cut out of Orange felt. Fold Beak in half along dashed lines and tack with needle and thread at each side; sew to Head.

With long end, sew Wings to each side of Head.

With long end, sew Head to center of Blanket.

BEAK DIAGRAM

Owl

◼◼◻◻ EASY +

Approximate Finished Size: Blanket - 12" (30.5 cm) square

SHOPPING LIST

Yarn (Medium Weight) 🧶4

[3.5 ounces, 170 yards
(100 grams, 156 meters) per skein]:

☐ Aqua - 1 skein

☐ Lt Green - 1 skein

Knitting Needles

Straight,

☐ Size 9 (5.5 mm) (for Blanket)

Double pointed (set of 4),

☐ Size 8 (5 mm) (for Head & Wings)

Additional Supplies

☐ Split ring marker

☐ Polyester fiberfill

☐ Brown embroidery floss

☐ Orange embroidery floss

☐ Tapestry needle

☐ Yarn needle

TECHNIQUES USED

- 🎥 M1 *(Figs. 3a & b, page 30)*
- 🎥 K2 tog *(Fig. 4, page 30)*
- 🎥 P3 tog *(Fig. 5, page 30)*

INSTRUCTIONS
Blanket

With straight knitting needles and Aqua, cast on 50 sts.

Row 1 (Right side): K1, purl across to last st, K1.

Row 2: K1, ★ 🎥 (K, P, K) **all** in the next st, P3 tog; repeat from ★ across to last st, K1.

Row 3: K1, purl across to last st, K1.

Row 4: K1, ★ P3 tog, (K, P, K) **all** in the next st; repeat from ★ across to last st, K1.

Repeat Rows 1-4 for pattern until piece measures approximately 11½" (29 cm) from cast on edge, ending by working Row 2 or Row 4.

Bind off all sts in pattern.

Head

With Lt Green, work same as Penguin, page 11, through Rnd 9; at end of Rnd 9, cut Lt Green: 42 sts.

With Aqua and beginning with Rnd 10, complete same as Penguin.

Wing (Make 2)

Wing is worked in rows on 2 double pointed needles.

With double pointed needles, using Lt Green and leaving an 8" (20.5 cm) end to sew Wing to Head, cast on 5 sts.

Rows 1 and 2: Knit across.

Row 3: K1, M1, K3, M1, K1: 7 sts.

Rows 4 and 5: Knit across.

Row 6: K1, (K2 tog, K1) twice: 5 sts.

Rows 7 and 8: Knit across.

Row 9: K1, K2 tog, K2: 4 sts.

Row 10: Knit across.

Row 11: K2 tog twice: 2 sts.

Bind off remaining sts in **knit**.

Finishing

Using photo as a guide:
With 🎥 outline stitch and Brown floss *(Figs. 7a and b, page 31)*, add U-shaped eyes to Head.
With 🎥 straight stitch and Orange floss *(Fig. 9, page 31)*, add upside-down triangle for beak; then fill triangle with 🎥 satin stitch *(Fig. 8, page 31)*.
With long end, sew Wings to each side of Head.
With long end, sew Head to center of Blanket.
Cut two 12" (30.5 cm) strands from both colors. Holding all 4 strands together, thread yarn needle. Insert needle at one side on top of Head, pulling yarn through until 3" (7.5 cm) is left; tie in a knot and trim ends. Repeat on opposite side of Head.

Puppy

▰▰▱▱ **EASY +**

Approximate Finished Size: Blanket - 12" (30.5 cm) square

TECHNIQUES USED

- YO (**Fig. 2, page 30**)
- M1 (**Figs. 3a & b, page 30**)
- K2 tog (**Fig. 4, page 30**)

INSTRUCTIONS
Blanket

With Tan, work same as Brown Bear, page 3.

Head

With double pointed needles, using Tan and leaving an 8" (20.5 cm) end to close cast on opening, cast on 8 sts; divide sts onto 3 needles (*see Using Double Pointed Needles, page 30*); place a marker to indicate the beginning of the round (*see Markers, page 29*).

Rnds 1 and 2: Knit around.

Rnd 3 (Increase rnd)**:** (K1, M1) around: 16 sts.

Rnd 4: Knit around.

Rnds 5 and 6: Repeat Rnds 3 and 4: 32 sts.

Rnd 7: (K2, M1) around: 48 sts.

Thread yarn needle with beginning end and weave through cast on edge; pull **tightly** to close opening, then secure end inside Head.

Rnds 8-11: Knit around.

Rnd 12 (Decrease rnd)**:** (K1, K2 tog) around: 32 sts.

Rnd 13: Knit around.

Rnd 14: (K2, K2 tog) around: 24 sts.

Row 15: Knit around.

Stuff Head lightly with polyester fiberfill.

Rows 16 and 17: Repeat Rnds 12 and 13: 16 sts.

Rnd 18: K2 tog around; cut yarn leaving a 12" (30.5 cm) end for sewing. 8 sts.

To gather the remaining sts, thread the yarn needle with the end and slip the remaining sts onto the yarn needle and yarn; pull **tightly** to close the hole and secure end, leaving the end long to sew to Blanket later.

Ear (Make 1 with Brown & 1 with Tan)

Ear is worked in rows on 2 double pointed needles.

With double pointed needles and leaving a 12" (30.5 cm) end to sew Ear to Head, cast on 4 sts.

Rows 1-3: Knit across.

Row 4: K2, M1, K2: 5 sts.

Rows 5-11: Knit across.

Row 12: K2, M1, K3: 6 sts.

Rnd 1 (Right side): Knit around.

Rnd 2: (K1, M1) around: 12 sts.

Bind off all sts in **knit**, leaving a long end for sewing.

Close cast on opening with beginning end.

Finishing

Using photo as a guide:
With 🎥 outline stitch and Black floss *(Figs. 7a & b, page 31)*, add U-shaped eyes to Brown Spot and Head. With long end, sew Brown Spot to Head. With 🎥 straight stitch and Brown floss *(Fig. 9, page 31)*, add upside-down triangle for Nose; then fill triangle with 🎥 satin stitch *(Fig. 8, page 31)*. With Brown floss, add remaining facial features with outline stitch and straight stitch. With long ends, sew Ears to Head, sewing the Brown Ear opposite the Brown Eye Spot.
With long end, sew Tan Spot to one Arm. Flatten top of Arms and sew to each side of Head with long end.
With long end, sew Head to center of Blanket.

Row 13: Knit across.

Row 14: K1, K2 tog twice, K1: 4 sts.

Row 15: K2 tog twice: 2 sts.

Bind off remaining sts in **knit**.

Arm (Make 2)

With double pointed needles, using Brown and leaving an 8" (20.5 cm) end to close cast on opening, cast on 11 sts; place a marker to indicate the beginning of the round.

Rnds 1-15: Knit around.

Bind off all sts in **knit**, leaving a long end for sewing.

Close cast on opening with beginning end.

Stuff Arm lightly with polyester fiberfill.

Spot (Make 1 with Brown & 1 with Tan)

With double pointed needles and leaving an 8" (20.5 cm) end to close cast on opening, cast on 6 sts; place a marker to indicate the beginning of the round.

Panda

EASY +

Approximate Finished Size: Blanket - 12" (30.5 cm) square

INSTRUCTIONS
Blanket

With straight knitting needles and White, cast on 56 sts.

Rows 1-3: Knit across.

Row 4: Purl across.

Row 5 (Right side)**:** K1, K2 tog 3 times, (YO, K1) 6 times, ★ K2 tog 6 times, (YO, K1) 6 times; repeat from ★ once **more**, K2 tog 3 times, K1.

Rows 6-9: Knit across.

Repeat Rows 4-9 for pattern until piece measures approximately 12" (30.5 cm) from cast on edge, ending by working Row 7.

Bind off all sts in **knit**.

Head

With White, work same as Puppy, page 19.

Eye Patch (Make 2)

With double pointed needles, using Black and leaving an 8" (20.5 cm) end to close cast on opening, cast on 6 sts; place a marker to indicate the beginning of the round.

Rnd 1 (Right side)**:** Knit around.

Rnd 2: (K1, M1) around: 12 sts.

Bind off all sts in **knit**, leaving a long end for sewing Eye Patch to Head.

Close cast on opening with beginning end.

Ear (Make 2)

With double pointed needles, using Black and leaving an 8" (20.5 cm) end to close cast on opening, cast on 6 sts; place a marker to indicate the beginning of the round.

Rnd 1 (Right side)**:** Knit around.

Rnd 2: (K1, M1) around: 12 sts.

Rnd 3: Knit around.

Bind off all sts in **knit**, leaving a long end for sewing Ear to Head.

Close cast on opening with beginning end.

Arm (Make 2)

With double pointed needles, using Black and leaving an 8" (20.5 cm) end to close cast on opening, cast on 11 sts; place a marker to indicate the beginning of the round.

Rnds 1-12: Knit around.

Bind off all sts in **knit**, leaving a long end for sewing.

Close cast on opening with beginning end.

Stuff Arm lightly with polyester fiberfill.

Finishing

Using photo as a guide:
With  backstitch and White floss *(Fig. 6, page 31)*, add circle to each Eye Patch. With long end, sew Eye Patches to Head.

With straight stitch and Black floss *(Fig. 9, page 31)*, add remaining facial features.
With long end, sew Ears to Head.
Flatten top of Arms and sew to each side of Head with long end.
With long end, sew Head to center of Blanket.

Kitten

EASY +

Approximate Finished Size: Blanket - 12" (30.5 cm) square

SHOPPING LIST

Yarn (Medium Weight)
[3.5 ounces, 170 yards
(100 grams, 156 meters) per skein]:
☐ Tan - 1 skein
[3 ounces, 145 yards
(85 grams, 133 meters) per skein]:
☐ Orange - 1 skein

Knitting Needles
Straight,
☐ Size 9 (5.5 mm) (for Blanket)
Double pointed (set of 4),
☐ Size 8 (5 mm) (for Head, Ears,
and Arms)

Additional Supplies
☐ Split ring marker
☐ Polyester fiberfill
☐ Brown embroidery floss
☐ Tapestry needle
☐ Yarn needle

TECHNIQUES USED
M1 (*Figs. 3a & b, page 30*)
K2 tog (*Fig. 4, page 30*)

INSTRUCTIONS
Blanket
With straight knitting needles and
Tan, cast on 50 sts.

Knit every row until piece measures
approximately 12" (30.5 cm) from
cast on edge.

Bind off all sts in **knit**.

Head
With Orange, work same as Puppy,
page 19.

Ear (Make 2)
Ear is worked in rows on 2 double
pointed needles.

With double pointed needles, using
Orange and leaving a 12" (30.5 cm)
end to sew Ear to Head, cast on 8 sts.

Rows 1-5: Knit across.

Row 6: K3, K2 tog, K3: 7 sts.

Row 7: K2, K2 tog twice, K1: 5 sts.

Row 8: Knit across.

Row 9: K1, K2 tog, K2: 4 sts.

Row 10: K2 tog twice: 2 sts.

Row 11: K2 tog: one st.

Cut yarn leaving a 6" (15 cm) end;
draw end through remaining st to
secure.

Arm (Make 2)
With double pointed needles, using
Orange and leaving an 8" (20.5 cm)
end to close cast on opening, cast on
11 sts; place a marker to indicate the
beginning of the round.

Rnds 1-13: Knit around.

Bind off all sts in **knit**, leaving a long
end for sewing.

Close cast on opening with beginning
end.

Stuff Arm lightly with polyester
fiberfill.

Finishing
Using photo as a guide:
With outline stitch and Brown
floss (*Figs. 7a & b, page 31*), add
U-shaped eyes to Head.
With straight stitch and
Brown floss (*Fig. 9, page 31*), add
upside-down triangle for Nose; then
fill triangle with satin stitch
(*Fig. 8, page 31*).
With straight stitch and Brown floss,
add remaining facial features.
With long ends, sew Ears to Head.
Flatten top of Arms and sew to each
side of Head with long end.
With long end, sew Head to center of
Blanket.

Giraffe

EASY +

Approximate Finished Size: Blanket - 12" (30.5 cm) square

INSTRUCTIONS

Blanket

With straight knitting needles and Lt Brown, cast on 52 sts.

Rows 1 and 2: Knit across.

Row 3: K2, purl across to last 2 sts, K2.

Row 4 (Right side)**:** Knit across.

Row 5: K2, P2, K2, (P6, K2) across to last 6 sts, P4, K2.

Row 6: (K6, P2) across to last 4 sts, K4.

Row 7: K2, purl across to last 2 sts, K2.

Row 8: Knit across.

Row 9: (K2, P6) across to last 4 sts, K4.

Row 10: K2, P2, (K6, P2) across to last 8 sts, K8.

Repeat Rows 3-10 for pattern until piece measures approximately 11¾" (30 cm) from cast on edge, ending by working Row 3 or Row 7.

Last 2 Rows: Knit across.

Bind off all sts in **knit**.

Head

With Lt Gold, work same as Puppy, page 19.

Snout

With double pointed needles, using Lt Gold and leaving an 16" (40.5 cm) end to sew Snout to Head, cast on 24 sts; place a marker to indicate the beginning of the round.

Rnds 1-3: Knit around.

Rnd 4: (K4, K2 tog) around: 20 sts.

Rnd 5: (K3, K2 tog) around: 16 sts.

Rnd 6: K2 tog around; cut yarn leaving an 8" (20.5 cm) end for sewing: 8 sts.

Thread yarn needle with the end and slip the remaining sts onto the yarn needle and yarn; pull **tightly** to close the hole and secure end inside Snout.

Stuff Snout lightly with polyester fiberfill.

Ear (Make 2)

Ear is worked in rows on 2 double pointed needles.

With double pointed needles, using Lt Gold and leaving an 8" (20.5 cm) end to sew Ear to Head, cast on 5 sts.

Rows 1 and 2: Knit across.

Row 3: (K2, M1) twice, K1: 7 sts.

Arm (Make 2)

With double pointed needles, using Lt Gold and leaving an 8" (20.5 cm) end to close cast on opening, cast on 11 sts; place a marker to indicate the beginning of the round.

Rnds 1-13: Knit around.

Bind off all sts in **knit**, leaving a long end for sewing.

Close cast on opening with beginning end.

Stuff Arm lightly with polyester fiberfill.

Rows 4 and 5: Knit across.

Row 6: K1, K2 tog twice, K2: 5 sts.

Row 7: Knit across.

Row 8: K1, K2 tog, K2: 4 sts.

Row 9: K2 tog twice: 2 sts.

Row 10: K2 tog: one st.

Cut yarn leaving a 6" (15 cm) end; draw end through remaining st to secure.

Horn (Make 2)

With double pointed needles, using Lt Gold and leaving an 8" (20.5 cm) end to sew Horn to Head, cast on 7 sts; place a marker to indicate the beginning of the round.

Rnds 1-6: Knit around; at end of Rnd 6, cut Lt Gold.

Rnds 7-9: With Lt Brown, knit around.

Cut yarn leaving an 8" (20.5 cm) end for sewing.

Thread yarn needle with the end and slip the remaining sts onto the yarn needle and yarn; pull **tightly** to close the hole and secure end inside Horn.

Stuff Horn lightly with polyester fiberfill.

Finishing

Using photo as a guide:

Sew Snout to Head.

With  outline stitch and Dk Brown floss *(Figs. 7a & b, page 31)*, add U-shaped eyes to Head.

With satin stitch and Dk Brown floss *(Fig. 8, page 31)*, add Nostrils to Snout.

With long ends, sew Ears and Horns to Head.

Flatten top of Arms and sew to each side of Head with long end.

With satin stitch, add Lt Brown spots to Head and Arms, if desired.

With long end, sew Head to center of Blanket.

GENERAL INSTRUCTIONS

ABBREVIATIONS

cm	centimeters
K	knit
M1	Make one
mm	millimeters
P	purl
Rnd(s)	Round(s)
st(s)	stitch(es)
tog	tog
YO	yarn over

SYMBOLS & TERMS

★ — work instructions following ★ as many **more** times as indicated in addition to the first time.

( ) or **[ ]** — work enclosed instructions **as many** times as specified by the number immediately following **or** work all enclosed instructions in the stitch indicated or contains explanatory remarks.

colon (:) — the number(s) given after a colon at the end of a row or round denote(s) the number of stitches you should have on that row or round.

GAUGE

Gauge is not of great importance; your Lovie may be a little larger or smaller without changing the overall effect.

MARKERS

As a convenience to you, we have used markers to mark the beginning of a round. Place a split ring marker around the first stitch in the round to indicate the beginning of the round. Move it up as the first stitch of each round is worked.

KNIT TERMINOLOGY		
UNITED STATES		**INTERNATIONAL**
gauge	=	tension
bind off	=	cast off
yarn over (YO)	=	yarn forward (yfwd) **or** yarn around needle (yrn)

◼◻◻◻ BEGINNER	Projects for first-time knitters using basic knit and purl stitches. Minimal shaping.
◼◼◻◻ EASY	Projects using basic stitches, repetitive stitch patterns, simple color changes, and simple shaping and finishing.
◼◼◼◻ INTERMEDIATE	Projects with a variety of stitches, such as basic cables and lace, simple intarsia, double-pointed needles and knitting in the round needle techniques, mid-level shaping and finishing.
◼◼◼◼ EXPERIENCED	Projects using advanced techniques and stitches, such as short rows, fair isle, more intricate intarsia, cables, lace patterns, and numerous color changes.

Yarn Weight Symbol & Names	LACE 0	SUPER FINE 1	FINE 2	LIGHT 3	MEDIUM 4	BULKY 5	SUPER BULKY 6	JUMBO 7
Type of Yarns in Category	Fingering, size 10 crochet thread	Sock, Fingering, Baby	Sport, Baby	DK, Light Worsted	Worsted, Afghan, Aran	Chunky, Craft, Rug	Super Bulky, Roving	Jumbo, Roving
Knit Gauge Ranges in Stockinette St to 4" (10 cm)	33-40 sts**	27-32 sts	23-26 sts	21-24 sts	16-20 sts	12-15 sts	7-11 sts	6 sts and fewer
Advised Needle Size Range	000 to 1	1 to 3	3 to 5	5 to 7	7 to 9	9 to11	11 to 17	17 and larger

* GUIDELINES ONLY: The chart above reflects the most commonly used gauges and needle sizes for specific yarn categories.

** Lace weight yarns are usually knitted on larger needles to create lacy openwork patterns. Accordingly, a gauge range is difficult to determine. Always follow the gauge stated in your pattern.

USING DOUBLE POINTED NEEDLES

Cast on required number of stitches onto one needle. Divide the stitches into thirds and slip one-third of the stitches onto each of 3 double pointed needles *(Fig. 1a)*, forming a triangle. With the fourth needle, knit across the stitches on the first needle *(Fig. 1b)*. You will now have an empty needle with which to knit the stitches from the next needle. Work the first stitch of each needle firmly to prevent gaps.

Fig. 1a

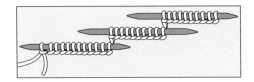

Fig. 1b

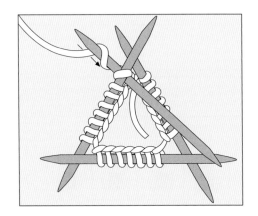

INCREASES

YARN OVER *(abbreviated YO)*

Bring the yarn forward **between** the needles, then back **over** the top of the right hand needle, so that it is now in position to knit the next stitch *(Fig. 2)*.

Fig. 2

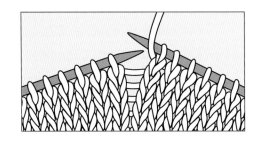

MAKE ONE *(abbreviated M1)*

Insert the **left** needle under the horizontal strand between the stitches from the **front** *(Fig. 3a)*. Then knit into the **back** of the strand *(Fig. 3b)*.

Fig. 3a

Fig. 3b

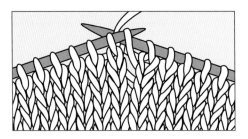

DECREASES

KNIT 2 TOGETHER

(abbreviated K2 tog)

Insert the right needle into the front of the first two stitches on the left needle as if to **knit** *(Fig. 4)*, then **knit** them together as if they were one stitch.

Fig. 4

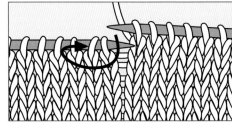

PURL 3 TOGETHER

(abbreviated P3 tog)

Insert the right needle into the **front** of the first three stitches on the left needle as if to **purl** *(Fig. 5)*, then **purl** them together as if they were one stitch.

Fig. 5

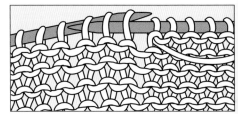

EMBROIDERY STITCHES

BACKSTITCH

The backstitch is worked from **right** to **left**. Come up at 1, go down at 2 and come up at 3 *(Fig. 6)*. The second stitch is made by going down at 1 and coming up at 4.

Fig. 6

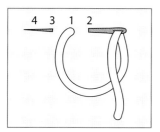

OUTLINE STITCH

Bring needle up at 1, leaving an end to be woven in later. Holding floss **above** the thumb, insert needle down at 2 and up again at 3 (halfway between 1 and 2) *(Fig. 7a)*; pull through. Insert needle down at 4 and up again at 2, making sure floss is **above** needle *(Fig. 7b)*; pull through.

Fig. 7a

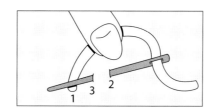

Fig. 7b

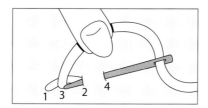

SATIN STITCH

Satin stitch is a series of straight stitches worked side-by-side so they touch but do not overlap. Come up at odd numbers and go down at even numbers *(Fig. 8)*.

Fig. 8

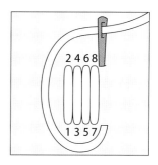

STRAIGHT STITCH

Straight stitch is just what the name implies, a single, straight stitch. Come up at 1 and go down at 2 *(Fig. 9)*.

Fig. 9

KNITTING NEEDLES																			
U.S.	0	1	2	3	4	5	6	7	8	9	10	10½	11	13	15	17	19	35	50
U.K.	13	12	11	10	9	8	7	6	5	4	3	2	1	00	000	---	---	---	---
Metric - mm	2	2.25	2.75	3.25	3.5	3.75	4	4.5	5	5.5	6	6.5	8	9	10	12.75	15	19	25

YARN INFORMATION

The Lovies in this book were made using Medium Weight Yarn with the exception of the Lamb which also uses a Super Bulky Weight Yarn. Any brand of the specified weight of yarn may be used. It is best to refer to the yardage/meters when determining how many balls or skeins to purchase. Remember, to arrive at the finished size, it is the GAUGE/TENSION that is important not the brand of yarn.

For your convenience, listed below are the specific yarns used to create our photography models. Because yarn manufacturers make frequent changes in their product lines, you may sometimes find it necessary to use a substitute yarn or to search for the discontinued product at alternate suppliers (locally or online).

BROWN BEAR
Lion Brand® Vanna's Choice®
Brown - #126 Chocolate
Tan - #123 Beige

BUNNY
Lion Brand® Vanna's Choice®
White - #100 White
Pink - #101 Pink
Red Heart® Super Saver®
Orange - #3251 Flame
Green - #672 Spring Green

LAMB
Lion Brand® Wool-Ease®
Natural - #098 Natural Heather
Grey - #151 Grey Heather
Lion Brand® Heartland® Thick & Quick®
Tan - #098 Acadia

PENGUIN
Lion Brand® Vanna's Choice®
White - #100 White
Black - #153 Black

DUCK
Lion Brand® Vanna's Choice®
Yellow - #157 Radiant Yellow
White - #100 White

OWL
Lion Brand® Vanna's Choice® Baby
Aqua - #102 Aqua
Lt Green - #168 Mint

PUPPY
Lion Brand® Vanna's Choice®
Tan - #123 Beige
Brown - #126 Chocolate

PANDA
Lion Brand® Vanna's Choice®
White - #100 White
Black - #153 Black

KITTEN
Lion Brand® Vanna's Choice®
Tan - #123 Beige
Orange - #306 Tangerine Mist

GIRAFFE
Lion Brand® Vanna's Choice®
Lt Brown - #130 Honey
Red Heart® Super Saver®
Lt Gold - #320 Cornmeal

Meet the Designer: Yolanda Soto-Lopez

Yolanda Soto-Lopez shares her crafting passion with her All Crafts Channel patterns and online videos for crochet, knitting, sewing, jewelry and other fun crafts. Find them on YouTube, Facebook, Ravelry.com, and through her website at allcraftschannel.com. "My goal is to take what seems hard and simplify it so everyone can have success," she says. "I believe that if you're not having fun then it's not worth doing. Let's Get the Party Started!"

We have made every effort to ensure that these instructions are accurate and complete. We cannot, however, be responsible for human error, typographical mistakes, or variations in individual work.

Production Team: Instructional/Technical Writer - Linda A. Daley; Editorial Writer - Susan Frantz Wiles; Senior Graphic Artist - Lora Puls; Graphic Artist - Frances Huddleston; Photo Stylist - Lori Wenger; and Photographer - Jason Masters.